Five Keys

for

Raising Boys

GREGORY L. JANTZ, PHD
WITH ANN MCMURRAY

AspirePress

Carson, California

AspirePress

Five Keys to Raising Boys
Copyright © 2016 Gregory L. Jantz
All rights reserved.
Aspire Press, an imprint of Rose Publishing, Inc.
17909 Adria Maru Lane
Carson, CA 90746 USA
www.aspirepress.com

Register your book at www.rose-publishing.com/register
and receive a FREE *How to Study the Bible* PDF
to print for your personal or ministry use.

Printed in the United States of America
010516RRD

Contents

Blue Is Not Pink 5

Key #1 Understanding a
Boy's Differences 13

Key #2 Guiding a Boy's Behavior 33

Key #3 Shielding a Boy's Heart 55

Key #4 Overseeing a Boy's Academics 71

Key #5 Educating a Boy about Sex 89

Word of Encouragement 105

Notes 108

Blue *Is* Not Pink

"*They're* just so different!" I was working with a frazzled mother, who was trying to juggle home, parenting, and work responsibilities. Asked about her children, she told me she had two—an eight-year-old girl and a five-year-old boy. That's when she blurted out the source of her frustration: the differences between them.

She went on to say that her daughter was a compliant child who listened and sought to please. Her son, however, was anything but compliant. He was in a constant state of motion and rarely stopped long enough to listen to her. Her daughter was quiet; her son was loud. Her daughter read books and spent hours playing with a large dollhouse constructed by a family member. Her son kicked balls in the house, spread out board games all over the kitchen table, and created forts with couch cushions and pillows.

Keeping up with him was exhausting. She wondered aloud, "Why isn't my son more like my daughter? Is there something wrong with him?"

I had to smile, because at the time I had two young boys at home myself. I knew exactly what she was describing. "There's nothing wrong with your son," I remember assuring her. "He's not broken; he's a boy."

The Pendulum *of* Preference

Pendulums are funny things, especially when they're part of social trends. For hundreds, if not thousands, of years, the social pendulum was permanently stuck in a position that benefited males, the standard by which both genders were judged.

About fifty years ago that pendulum of preference began to swing differently. Instead of finding a happy medium between characteristics of both genders, there is now little acknowledgment that there are differences between boys and girls. And where a difference is perceived, the female characteristic seems to be preferred.

I grew up in a time when conventional wisdom said that boys and girls were essentially the same, except for male and female plumbing. Any differences between the way girls reacted and boys reacted was said to be *nurture*—how that child was raised within the family and society. *Nature* was said to be neutral, treating both boys and girls the same. Girls were said to act like girls, not because of nature, but because they were nurtured as girls by those around them. Boys acted like boys, not because maleness was their nature, but because society treated them as boys.

Complement Not Compete

While I still believe a portion of that to be true—that we do treat boys and girls differently—I also have come to believe nurture isn't all there is to the differences between boys and girls. Boys and girls are different, not only because society treats them differently, but also because they were *made* differently. Male and female outsides are different, as well as their insides, especially the insides of their brains. The last twenty-five years have produced brain research that shows several marked differences in the ways male and female brains develop and react.

NURTURE ISN'T ALL THERE IS TO THE DIFFERENCES BETWEEN BOYS AND GIRLS

Having grown up in a household with a sister, I intuitively understood that boys and girls are different. However, the issue became more urgent with the births of my sons. Society did treat them differently, and that difference wasn't always positive. At one point, my wife and I had a school representative suggest that one of my sons needed to be on medication because he was acting, as far as I could tell, like a normal boy. Through that personal experience, I began to do research on what was happening to boys in schools and in society.

My research led me to Michael Gurian, the founder of the Gurian Institute, which provides training and coaching services to close the gender achievement gap. For several decades, Michael has been doing his own studies of the condition of boys and how boys and girls think and act differently. He has written several excellent books on the subject. A few years ago, we collaborated on a book together, *Raising Boys by Design*.[1] As we worked together, I came to truly appreciate his research and wisdom on the subject of gender differences.

> As human beings, we are created to be equal but different.
>
> "SO GOD CREATED MANKIND IN HIS OWN IMAGE, IN THE IMAGE OF GOD HE CREATED THEM; MALE AND FEMALE HE CREATED THEM."
> —GENESIS 1:27

According to Michael, the condition of boys in society has deteriorated. He said recently, "I just traveled to Washington, D.C., to brief Congress members on our boys crisis, because I have been a child advocate for thirty years and never been more worried about our boys than I am now."[2] The societal pendulum of gender issues appears to have moved toward another extreme: this time, to the detriment of boys.

Blue and pink are not the same. Male and female are not the same. As human beings, we are created to be equal but different. Genesis 1:27 says, "So God created mankind in his own image, in the image of God he created them; male and female he created them."

BOYS MAY NOT ACT LIKE GIRLS BUT THEY ARE NOT BROKEN

I, for one, am glad for the diversity of God. "If the whole body were an eye, where would the sense of hearing be? If the whole body were an ear, where would the sense of smell be?" (1 Corinthians 12:17). In God's design of the body, eyes and ears and noses are not created to compete against each other but to complement each other.

In God's design of boys and girls, male and female, I believe the same holds true.

Those of you who work with and love boys, please take heart. Those boys may not act like girls—at home, at school, at play—but they are not broken. Science is providing fascinating insights into the mysteries of human development. We are learning how very much alike we are and also how diverse the sexes are. The more we know, the more we understand the nature of both our boys and our girls and how to honor that nature through the ways we parent our children and interact with all children.

KEY #1:

Understanding *a* Boy's Differences

The following quotes are from women who were caught by surprise when it comes to mothering boys.

■ "I certainly didn't push my son toward trucks and my daughter toward tutus. If anything, I went out of my way to avoid giving them gender-stereotyped toys, offering glittery finger paint to my son and trains to my daughter. But it didn't matter: My son turned his doll's crib into a race car and my daughter was obsessed with shoes."[3]

■ "In my pre-mommy days, I envisioned myself like Marmee in *Little Women*: the wise, loving lead of a feminine brood. My fantasy seem[ed] poised to come true with the birth of our firstborn, Hannah, a calm and compliant child who was snuggly, easily entertained, and loved every hairdo I concocted for her. . . . When Hannah turned 3, my *Little Women* fantasy came to an abrupt halt with the birth of Isaac, followed 16 months later by Benny. From the moment my first son was born, I was scared silly about the task at hand; I imagined wildness, loudness, adoration of trucks, and risk-taking behavior that would end in visits to the ER."[4]

- "When you have a girl, you know that you can always fall back on your own childhood memories to guide you as a parent. But unless you grew up with a brother, there's a good chance that parts of raising a boy can take you by surprise."[5]

- "It seems, too, boys are always on a mission— competing in some dire, fantasy face-off. For reasons unknown, restaurant outings seem to beckon their invisible foes, as breadsticks become makeshift swords and crayons instant torpedoes. . . . Did I mention boys are fans of water pistols, pools, and puddles, yet less fond of bathing? . . . What's more, boys will jump off anything and approach running and climbing with Olympic fervor."[6]

■ ■ ■

Boys Will Be Boys

When I was growing up, there was a saying "Boys will be boys." This saying was usually repeated right after a boy or group of boys engaged in some sort of rowdy or rambunctious behavior. Whether or not the saying evoked humor or anger might be connected to whether or not your personal property had been damaged! This saying was just one way to rationalize some of the crazy things boys would do.

However, not all boys are equally rowdy, and they don't all act in the same ways. But when it comes to the brain itself, scientists are finding there are developmental and structural differences between the male brain and the female brain. It's probably no surprise to parents of boys to learn that boys' and girls' brains are just ...*different*.

Gray *and* White

I'm not a brain expert by any means, but I've come to understand a few important concepts. Brains of both genders utilize neural tissue called matter, which comes in two forms—*gray matter* and *white matter*. Male brains appear to use more of their gray matter for mental processing, while female brains use more of their white matter to make connections between the different parts of the brain that are processing information.

So, as I've come to understand it, boys tend to use gray matter to focus on a task with singular concentration, while white matter allows girls to incorporate multiple factors and, in essence, connect the dots between them. Research continues as to the reasons and consequences of the differences between gray and white matter and how each is utilized, but what research has shown so far is that the brains of boys and girls are clearly not identical. While they are similar in an array of ways, they are also decidedly different. (It should be noted that although boys and girls use their brains differently, neither is more intelligent than the other.)[7]

Waffles *and* Spaghetti

Brain research can be difficult for many people to comprehend. I tend to do better with concrete visuals. Although you cannot generalize about all men or all women—everyone is a bit different—one analogy I've particularly found helpful over the years compared men (or male brains) to waffles and women (or female brains) to spaghetti.[8] In this analogy, each man is like a waffle on a plate. That one waffle is made up of many distinct boxes, and each man has a tendency to camp out in a single box, highly focused on whatever activity is inside that box. In order to move from task to task, he must make the effort to climb out of one box and into another. The effort is not seamless. A woman, on the other hand, is like spaghetti on a plate. The noodles intertwine and connect with each other, allowing for relatively easy transition from one activity to another.

I've seen this in my own life. I can be talking to my wife, LaFon, about one situation, and she has the capacity to bring in four or five additional details from things she's learned that provide context and contribute to the discussion. Her ability to connect the dots is amazing. On the other hand, if I'm in the midst of concentrating on a task, the building could fall down around me and I'd probably be unaware.

WHEN BOYS ARE ENGAGED FULLY IN A TASK, THEY DEVELOP TUNNEL VISION.

I remember talking to a female friend who became convinced that her husband was routinely ignoring her. In the evening, after spending the day apart, she would want to catch up with her husband or talk through a problem. Often, however, if her husband was watching television or reading, he would "ignore" her. Though she repeatedly said his name, he wouldn't respond. She naturally assumed that he heard her and was making a conscious choice to disregard her, which she found incredibly irritating.

I doubted this man was intentionally ignoring his wife. "He's not ignoring you," I suggested. "He's probably just concentrating on whatever he's doing."

She seemed shocked at the idea that he wasn't able to switch gears, as she called it, as easily and quickly as she could. Somewhat embarrassed, she even confessed to counting seconds in her head, waiting to see how long it would take for him to pay attention to her. The more time it took, the angrier she became. Needless to say, this was causing difficulties in their marriage.

It appears that when boys—or men—are engaged fully in a task, they develop a sort of tunnel vision. This ability to concentrate has some advantages, as it allows for minimal disruption due to distractions and, presumably, increased productivity. Hyperfocus can be helpful, unless you're the person trying to break through that wall of concentration.

Just watch a boy engaged in a video game.[9] His ability to focus is admirable and if called for homework or dinner, he may simply fail to respond. Is he being disrespectful? Perhaps, but perhaps not. Maybe he's being focused and acting according to his nature. Of course, you still need to get his attention.

So how can you work within this nature?

- **GET HIS ATTENTION VISUALLY.**

  When he's focused and says he didn't hear you, he probably didn't. Instead of calling out to him from behind his back, walk into his line of sight and say, "I need to talk with you. Can you give me your attention?"

- **GIVE HIM MORE TIME TO TRANSITION.**

  Because he can get "stuck" in a single task, moving from one thing to another may not happen as quickly for him as for a girl.

- **GIVE HIM A DEADLINE.**

  He may say "Just a minute" when asked to disengage, but to him, a minute may not have the same meaning it has for you. In that case, go back and remind him to climb out of his task box of video gaming (or homework or reading or whatever) and transition into the task you have for him.

■ UNDERSTAND REPETITION.

To you, he may be on that video game for what seems like an hour, doing the same thing over and over again. To him, however, by playing that same game level for an hour, he's learning every single time he tries and fails. He's not wasting an hour doing the same thing over and over; he's making progress on accomplishing his goal.

Constant Motion

One study says that male brains are designed to connect perception and coordinated action, while female brains are designed to communicate between analytical and intuitive mental processing.[10] In other words, boys relate to the world through motion.

"On average, boys do show higher activity levels than girls from infancy onward. They are more likely to engage in outdoor play, rough play, and activities that cover large areas of physical space."[11] Boys build forts and run nonstop, gobbling up play space. They jump and flail their arms. They experience their world by moving through it.

Boys tend to have greater spatial skills. They are better at mentally manipulating objects in space (a skill called mental rotation). Boys also tend to have an advantage with embedded figures recognition, which gauges a person's ability to find geometric shapes in larger designs. When boys get older, this spatial acuity means they can exhibit greater navigation skills, like map reading.[12] Is it any wonder that boys spend so much time in motion, rotating themselves through physical space? Space is the air they breathe—the way they are wired to interpret the world.

This tendency toward energy and spatial skills may be what gives boys a sense of adventure. "Boys are more likely to handle a new object physically; girls are more likely to use visual exploration, looking carefully at a novel object without actually touching it. Interestingly, male and female infants show different reactions when left alone to explore. Boys are more likely to explore objects and become more independent."[13]

Busy boys move through space as they discover and conquer their worlds. This motion and movement, especially in a confined space or at an inappropriate time, can seem disruptive or even disrespectful. But the boy is simply acting out of his nature.

So how can you adjust for this constant movement?

■ ENCOURAGE PHYSICAL EXPLORATION.

Whenever possible, get a boy outside and involved in hands-on exploration. In addition to giving him a book about bugs, take him outside and have him look for and handle bugs. Teach him about circumference or diameter by letting him measure objects. Remember, male brains are designed to connect perception with action, so he may understand the concepts better when he is experiencing them physically.

■ CREATE TIMES FOR A BOY TO MOVE.

Every boy needs to learn self-control and when it is appropriate to engage in physical movement. Just as you wouldn't expect a puppy to develop well if always kept in a cage, a boy may not develop well if constantly contained and confined. There are times to sit quietly, but there are also times to run and play and jump and yell. He will have an easier time doing the former if you give him time to do the latter.

■ CREATE SPACES FOR A BOY TO MOVE.

Not everyone has the square footage that works best for many boys. If that's the case, be sure to plan time for large-space play, whether that is in an indoor play space or an outdoor park or field.

■ LET HIM WEAR HIMSELF OUT.

He's got energy, so let him use it. If you attempt to keep that energy bottled up, contained, and directed toward nonactive play, that energy is going to come out somewhere.

■ PLAY GAMES THAT TAKE ADVANTAGE OF HIS STRENGTHS.

He's spatial-oriented, so choose games that involve manipulating objects through space. Any toy that involves large movements (cars and trucks, for example, or even spaceships) are great for this.

The flip side of a boy fully engaged in activity is a boy fully engaged at rest.

"[JESUS] SAID TO THEM, 'COME WITH ME BY YOURSELVES TO A QUIET PLACE AND GET SOME REST.'"
—MARK 6:31

The flip side of a boy fully engaged in activity is a boy fully engaged at rest. This is another fascinating difference between male and female brains. Male brains can more easily transition from a state of activity to a state of inactivity. Some have called this state of inactivity *zoning out*. When zoning out, male brains have the capacity to go into a blank box and stay there.

So how do you deal with boys and their zoning out?

■ LEARN TO RECOGNIZE THE REST STATE OF A BOY.

This may sound like a contradiction, but male brains appear to recharge and renew themselves by, in essence, turning off most of the lights. I guess I would compare this to the sleep setting on a computer. The screen is blank, but the computer is still operational, conserving energy that will be needed the next time it's activated.

■ ALLOW A BOY TO KEEP HIMSELF ACTIVATED.

A boy will usually know when he's zoning out and may use his body to keep his mind engaged. He may tap his fingers or a pencil. He may fidget in his chair. Sometimes, these behaviors can appear to indicate the boy is not paying attention when, in reality, these behaviors are used by the boy to maintain his attention and avoid dipping into a rest state.

■ **ALLOW A BOY TIME TO POWER BACK UP.**

Male brains simply seem to need more time to come back up out of a rest state. This rest state can happen while the boy is doing something else. He may be watching television one moment and in the next, zone out for a moment, as he recharges his mental batteries. The transition back to fully alert may take longer to accomplish than for a girl, so be patient.

Cross Talk—Boys' Verbal Ability

There are two hemispheres in the brain—the right and the left—and female brains appear to have more cross-talk between those two sides, which may translate into females having greater verbal skills. "Researchers, using brain imaging technology that captures blood flow to 'working' parts of the brain, analyzed how men and women process language. All subjects listened to a novel. When males listened, only the left hemisphere of their brains was activated. The brains of female subjects, however, showed activity on both the left and right hemispheres."[14] Studies show that at an earlier age, girls tend to be more verbal, develop complex language skills, and utilize a larger vocabulary than boys.[15]

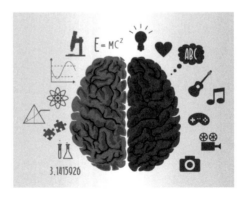

Compared to girls, many boys might be considered slower to develop verbal skills and have a smaller and less complex vocabulary. However, if you only compare boys to boys, then their verbal skills, vocabulary acquisition, and language usage will be right on track. Taking more time to develop language skills and vocabulary does not mean that boys are any less intelligent than girls. On average, boys just develop different skills at different times than girls.

So how do you encourage boys' verbal skills?

■ BE PATIENT TO TEACH PATIENCE.

A boy who is having difficulty articulating what he needs or thinks may exhibit irritation, frustration, or anger. He may slap his forehead, grit his teeth, or punch the air out of frustration when verbal expression does not happen as fast

In order to teach him to be patient with himself, you first should be patient with him.

"THEREFORE, AS GOD'S CHOSEN PEOPLE, HOLY AND DEARLY LOVED, CLOTHE YOURSELVES WITH COMPASSION, KINDNESS, HUMILITY, GENTLENESS AND PATIENCE."
—COLOSSIANS 3:12

or easily as physical expression. In order to teach him to be patient with himself, you first should be patient with him.

■ HELP ENCOURAGE THE USE OF WORDS.

Children, in general, can become adept at obtaining what they want through the easiest means necessary. For boys, that may mean a physical gesture, instead of a spoken request. Help a boy use his words and develop new ones by, for example, making sure he gives an understandable verbal request.

TAKING MORE TIME TO DEVELOP LANGUAGE SKILLS AND VOCABULARY DOES NOT MEAN THAT BOYS ARE ANY LESS INTELLIGENT THAN GIRLS.

■ ENCOURAGE VERBAL EXPRESSION WITH PHYSICAL MOVEMENT.

One of the best ways to encourage a boy to talk is to get him involved in a physical activity and engage him in conversation about what is happening. For example, if he is building a tower, start asking him questions about the tower: Who is in it? Why was it built? What will happen if the tower is knocked down? Help him to incorporate verbal expression along with his natural physical expression.

■ PROVIDE WORD OPTIONS IF HE'S HAVING TROUBLE EXPRESSING HIMSELF.

Because his verbal skills take longer to develop, he may not have the word he needs to express what he wants or feels. Provide him with options and allow him to make his own choices.

Differences *and* Choices

As more and more research demonstrates the differences between males and females, boys and girls, each person has to make choices.

- Do I acknowledge those differences or do I attempt to act as if they don't really exist?

- If I acknowledge that male and female differences exist, what am I to do with those differences?

- Social structures in the past have taken those differences and created a male preference, to the detriment of females. Do I reverse the pendulum and create a female preference, to the detriment of boys?

As a Christian, I believe God created people as male and female, with differences and without preference. As neurologist Ruben Gur has said, "Most of these differences are complementary. They increase the chances of males and females joining together. It helps the whole species."[16] God did not create different genders to create confusion, competition, and chaos, "for God is not a God of disorder but of peace" (I Corinthians 14:33). Instead, I believe, God created different and complementary genders with great similarities and also unique characteristics, behaviors, and physiology. When I see these differences, I see the complexity and diversity of creation. *Vive la différence!*

> God did not create
> different genders
> to create confusion,
> competition, and chaos,
>
> "FOR GOD IS NOT A GOD OF
> DISORDER BUT OF PEACE"
> —1 CORINTHIANS 14:33

KEY #2:

Guiding *a* Boy's Behavior

When I was in sixth grade, my family moved from Dodge City, Kansas, to Boise, Idaho. We moved in the middle of that school year and I wound up going to a school with a less-than-stellar reputation. Being the new kid, a group of boys at the school decided to put me in my place. I, on the other hand, didn't like where they wanted to put me, so I got into fights on a regular basis. Between fights, my grades dropped and I found myself drawn to the group of kids who liked to smoke on the corner rather than attend school. When I hit junior high, it seemed as if I spent more time in the principal's office than in class. I didn't get much out of junior high except a memorable three-day suspension.

My parents, understandably, were concerned and tried a variety of ways to get me turned around. The summer before high school, they sent me to a church camp about a hundred miles north of Boise. I wasn't thrilled about going and proved it by my behavior. I put firecrackers in the nightly campfire and became the kid the adults at camp were told to watch.

One camp counselor, Mort, a guy in his thirties, did watch me; he also watched out for me. He'd come up behind me and say things like "Gregg, I believe in you." I thought he was weird, maybe even a stalker, because he kept turning up whenever I was, giving me encouragement.

In school, I didn't participate in sports, unless you counted unsupervised fighting, but Mort began to encourage me to run in the traditional end-of-camp cross-country race. "I believe in you," he kept saying. "You'll do well." I decided to run the race out of sheer frustration and anger at Mort. I didn't believe he was serious and I wanted to shove the race in his face.

I started out angry, but at some point during the race, that anger changed. I'd started running to show Mort how mad I was. I kept running to show Mort how good I was. I was mad at Mort for believing in me and yet somehow glad he did, because I hadn't believed in myself for a long time. So I ran as hard as I could and made it across the finish line, not realizing I'd come in first.

That summer changed me. In junior high, I was the kid who got into fights, the kid adults were told to look out for. By my senior year in high school, I was named outstanding student of the year. Mort, and the lesson he taught me—the power you can harness when you believe in yourself—has stayed with me all these years. As I began to do research on boys and experience being a boy fresh through my sons, I had to wonder what were the lessons being given to boys today. Many of those lessons do *not* give boys the encouragement of "I believe in you."

■ ■ ■

Recognize His Capacity *for* Character

"A growing share of American men are in trouble—the most serious trouble they have been in since World War II. They are disengaging from all of the traditional roles that have defined successful male lives for thousands of years: from work, from married life and families, from civic life, and from education. For the first time in our nation's history, our sons are less educated than their fathers. Now a growing share of men are imprisoned, killing themselves or living in poverty."[17] This dismal analysis—that boys are growing up to be men who, as a group, are struggling—is not unique in research regarding the state of boys in our culture.

I DESPERATELY WANTED TO BE SOMEONE ELSE BUT DIDN'T KNOW HOW TO GET THERE.

While the reasons for the decline of male success in this country are complex, I firmly believe that part of the decline has to do with a society that finds its preferences out of sync with boys and their nature. When I was having trouble in junior high, I suppose I was a classic "tough case." I was tanking academically, involved in fights, and disrespectful and disobedient to adults. On the outside,

I was headed for failure. On the inside, however, I desperately wanted to be someone else but didn't know how to get there. Then Mort took the time to look beyond the outside and invest in the inside of that young boy. Mort took the time to let me know I had the capacity to become a man of character.

I love this description of character: "Character is forged on the anvil of self-discipline. Character is gained experience by experience, decision by decision, lesson by lesson. Character isn't something that can only be talked out, memorized, and recited. Character has to be lived out courageously."[18] This description echoes the words of the apostle Paul: "We also glory in our sufferings, because know that suffering produces perseverance; perseverance, character; and character, hope" (Romans 5:3–4).

Perhaps there is no area where hope and courage are needed more than for today's boys to claim their destiny

> Boys don't need to grow up to become less like boys; boys need to grow up to become more like men.
>
> "BE WATCHFUL, STAND FIRM IN THE FAITH, ACT LIKE MEN, BE STRONG. LET ALL THAT YOU DO BE DONE IN LOVE."
> —1 CORINTHIANS 16:13–14, ESV

of manhood in a culture that can view that arrival with suspicion. Boys need to know that becoming a man is a positive rite of passage, a desired and valued state of adulthood and responsibility.

Culture may be at odds with manhood, but God is not. I love this admonition: "Be watchful, stand firm in the faith, act like men, be strong. Let all that you do be done in love" (1 Corinthians 16:13–14, ESV). Boys don't need to grow up to become less like boys; boys need to grow up to become more like men.

Encourage His Inner Hero

I love the image of a boy flying through the room with a makeshift cape sailing out behind him. Boys desire to be seen and to act as strong and courageous—as superheroes. Boys want to be challenged and taught how to respond with character, especially in difficult situations. They long to prove themselves worthy of respect, both within boy culture and in the culture at large.

I believe stories about heroes are important, because they generally involve some key components:

- an ordinary person who is able to act extraordinarily;

- a test of character—a time when the person must decide to act honorably or dishonorably within a true temptation;

- and a prize to be won.

These stories exist all around us. We can use them as avenues to engage boys in thinking about the courage and heroics needed to successfully transition into manhood and become men of character.

Through Scripture

I believe the Bible is the foundational source for heroic stories and the lessons they teach, from the Garden of Eden to the Garden of Gethsemane. Adam, Abraham, Isaac, Jacob, David, Solomon, Samuel, Sampson—the list continues to Peter, Paul, John, and, ultimately, Jesus. A boy needs to identify with male role models as he learns what being a successful, loving, and caring man means.

I believe adults can gain a fresh perspective on age-old biblical stories when viewed through the eyes, hearts, and minds of boys. When reading about a mighty battle or work of faith, boys can be encouraged to engage in role-playing, acting out the story. As a part of this role-playing, conversation can be used to personalize and claim the story and its lessons:

- What is good about the main person?

- What is the person trying to do?

- Why is doing the right thing hard for the person?

- Did the person do what was right in this situation?

- What would you do, if you were in the same situation?

- Have you been able to act in a similar way?

- How could you act in a similar way in the future?

The Bible is full of stories of ordinary people doing extraordinary things by the strength and grace of God. Boys need to know that they are no different from those ordinary people in Scripture. They, too, can be faithful and obedient to God and watch extraordinary things of God be done through them. "He has told you, O man, what is good; and what does the LORD require of you but to do justice, and to love kindness, and to walk humbly with your God?" (Micah 6:8,

> **Boys can watch God do extraordinary things through them.**
>
> "HE HAS TOLD YOU, O MAN, WHAT IS GOOD; AND WHAT DOES THE LORD REQUIRE OF YOU BUT TO DO JUSTICE, AND TO LOVE KINDNESS, AND TO WALK HUMBLY WITH YOUR GOD?"
> —MICAH 6:8, ESV

ESV). God has a purpose for each boy—a noble and heroic purpose. Boys need to understand this destiny awaits them, and they need help to grow and discover that destiny.

Through Media

Lessons of struggle, perseverance, character, strength, and hope are found not only in Scripture but also in culture. There are movies, books, and video games that capture the essence of heroism and can capture the heart of a boy. Even flawed cultural offerings can provide an opportunity to instill character-building traits in boys. You may, however, need to approach some of these offerings like eating fish: enjoy the meat, but be careful to pick out the bones.

■ VIDEO GAMES

Play with the boy, so you understand the context of the game. After play is over, engage him in conversation about the characters—their actions, attitudes, and ultimate outcomes. Find out which character the boy identifies with and why.

■ BOOKS

Especially for younger children, reading through a book or series of books together can be an enriching experience. Not only are you strengthening your relationship by spending time together, but you're also strengthening verbal skills and vocabulary usage.

● Don't restrict yourself to just what is popular at the moment. There are classic stories of danger and hardship. Do you remember the movie *The Princess Bride?* When a boy comes down with the flu, his grandfather arrives to read the boy a book. The boy is skeptical about this old-fashioned form of entertainment but reluctantly agrees to being read to. Of course, by the end, the boy is completely enthralled by the story and asks his grandfather to come back the next day and read it again.

This could be you. If you breezed through childhood without a clue about the classics, just google "best books for boys" or "classic books for boys" to begin your search for swashbuckling tales of danger and derring-do!

● Make sure reading together doesn't turn into the equivalent of a homework assignment. The goal is to allow the boy to become immersed in the story, not answer twenty questions every third page. When the goal is to enjoy the story as it unfolds, the conversations will come.

■ MOVIES

Generally, for younger boys, the most effective movies have a simple story with a straightforward dilemma or challenge that must be faced. However, don't underestimate the power of a heroic story for older boys. If you have any questions about the appropriateness of movies your boy may want to watch, consider consulting a website such as pluggedin.com for reviews from a biblical perspective. Older boys and teens are able, even eager, to stretch and test their understanding of suffering, perseverance, character, and hope. Movies can provide a conduit for this level of exploration.

Help Him Embrace Failure

Risk involves failure; how can there be risk if failure is not a possibility? Boys can be natural risk-takers. While they may profess loudly their assurance of success, inside the heart of the boy a seed of doubt can burrow.

What happens if I fail?

As a father, I want my sons to take risks because I find value in both success and failure. As a Christian, I want my sons to understand the reality of both, because Christians are neither guaranteed success or insulated from failure: "For though the righteous fall seven times, they rise again, but the wicked stumble when calamity strikes" (Proverbs 24:16). What do I learn from this passage about success and failure? I learn that calamity strikes the righteous as well as the wicked (or, as Matthew 5:45 tells us, the rain falls on the just and the unjust). When disaster strikes, both the righteous and wicked will fall. However, while the wicked stumble, the righteous rise again. I want my sons to understand that being a Christian does not dictate whether or not you fall; being a Christian dictates whether or not you rise.

> Christians are neither guaranteed success nor insulated from failure.
>
> "[GOD] CAUSES HIS SUN TO RISE ON THE EVIL AND THE GOOD, AND SENDS RAIN ON THE RIGHTEOUS AND THE UNRIGHTEOUS."
> —MATTHEW 5:45

As a father, I help my sons understand the value of both success and failure through the struggles they experience. I also teach them by sharing my own. Because I am mindful of keeping things age-appropriate for my sons, the older they become, the more I can share about my life and my past. Few things give me greater joy than watching my sons attain that "aha" moment by hearing about one of my personal struggles. When my sons learn not to repeat my mistakes, my bad experiences have been redeemed for a greater purpose.

USE FAILURES AS STEPPING STONES TO SUCCESS.

Successes and failures are a part of life. Instead of being something to avoid, use failures as stepping stones to success.

■ BE CLEAR ABOUT WHAT YOU SEE AS SUCCESS.

A boy desires to complete the tasks given to him, to be successful. When giving him something to accomplish, be specific about the conditions for success. Give detailed direction and then watch him rise to the challenge!

■ BE CLEAR ABOUT WHAT YOU SEE AS FAILURE.

Don't assume a boy will understand the parameters of failure unless you spell them out for him. Clear, unambiguous communication is best. For example, if you leave for several hours and merely call out "Clean your room!" on your way out the door, don't be surprised if that room is still a mess when you get back. Instead, explain, "I'm leaving for two hours and when I get back, I want you to have your bed made, your room straightened, and your dirty clothes taken to the laundry. If this does not happen, you will clean your room under my supervision and there will be no video games for the rest of the day." Now you have provided clear definitions of success and failure and the consequences of failure.

■ FOLLOW THROUGH.

You will do neither yourself nor a boy much good if you lay out consequences and then fail to follow through with them.

■ CELEBRATE SUCCESS.

Part of the reward for doing a good job is being acknowledged. This acknowledgment could be a verbal compliment, a fist bump, or a high five. Make sure to pay attention when things go right. Jesus says the angels throw a party in heaven when someone chooses to do what's right (Luke 15:7). I confess that too often with my sons I have overlooked their successes, treating them as mere givens, and saved my attention most often for when things go wrong. Sincere and genuine appreciation is needed by boys, and giving it reinforces the rewards of accomplishment and character.

■ PROTECT SELF-ESTEEM.

Sincere and genuine appreciation also reinforces self-esteem. There is an ongoing societal debate about the efficacy of participation trophies and the like. For younger boys, I have no problem with finding ways to celebrate the best in each boy. However, as a boy gets older, he becomes more aware of the meaning of success and failure. I remember feeling dishonest when I was overly praised for doing less than my best. Boys need to reach for lofty goals. When good-intentioned adults move those goals too easily within reach, a boy's ability to stretch can waste away. Giving him false praise does not guarantee he will end up feeling good about himself; sometimes, it guarantees the opposite.

> Jesus says the angels throw a party in heaven when someone chooses to do what's right.
>
> "I TELL YOU THAT IN THE SAME WAY THERE WILL BE MORE REJOICING IN HEAVEN OVER ONE SINNER WHO REPENTS THAN OVER NINETY-NINE RIGHTEOUS PERSONS WHO DO NOT NEED TO REPENT."
> —LUKE 15:7

■ INTEGRATE FAILURE.

- Whenever I find myself having to deal with failure, I try to remember that failure is not unusual. "For all have sinned and fall short of the glory of God" (Romans 3:23).

- Failure is an excellent teacher; failure teaches you what does not work.

- Our failures contribute to suffering, but as we know, suffering can lead to hope!

- My boys usually have reasons why they fail. My job as a parent is to help them understand why and how their choices produced negative outcomes—not so I can pound them into the ground for their stupidity or rebelliousness, but so I can motivate them to make a different choice the next time.

■ MOVE FROM WHAT TO WHY.

A younger boy will need help understanding what he's done wrong. For example, if a toddler becomes angry and kicks the cat, he needs to understand that action is wrong. The message to communicate is "Do not kick the cat." However, say the boy is older and knows "Do not kick the cat," but he kicks the cat anyway. Repeating "Do not kick the cat" isn't going to help him; he already knows that. Instead, help him understand why he kicked the cat. In doing this, you move from action to intention. Understanding intention transfers his focus from what is wrong on the outside (the cat was in the way) to what is wrong on the inside (the desire to strike out against something smaller and weaker). He can be reminded that true men do not do such a thing; on the contrary, true men seek to protect the smaller and weaker.

FAILURE IS AN EXCELLENT TEACHER; FAILURE TEACHES YOU WHAT DOES NOT WORK.

■ USE EXAMPLES FROM TEAMS AND SPORTS.

Boys can be competitive by nature and many will want to be a part of a team, whether through a sport or club or just a group in the neighborhood. Through these experiences, boys learn how to navigate competition, personal interactions, and fair play. Boys get what it means to be on a team, and this understanding can be used to illustrate other situations. For example, when helping a boy to understand why he is required to set the table, clean up after dinner, or do any number of chores, the family unit can be presented to him as a type of team. If he has trouble being motivated to brush his teeth at night, he can be reminded that he often must endure training exercises to learn a sport. Find ways to connect the dots within a context he understands and likes.

■ UTILIZE THE POWER OF "YET."

Use the word "yet" when talking with your son about an attempt that didn't succeed. "I know you're disappointed that you haven't mastered that skateboard trick *yet*." The implication of a verbal "yet" is that success is still attainable. It just might take a lot of hard work and many attempts to get there. "Yet" helps kids understand that effort and struggle can triumph over raw intelligence in many cases.

I believe boys want to succeed in life, yet they can find themselves challenged to know which paths to take. Boys want to be challenged and victorious, to do great things and change the world. Manhood, in our current climate, has taken a beating. Our parental duty is to rekindle the respect and value of masculinity. We must teach our boys the joys and challenges that await them as they grow unapologetically into men of character. Society may attempt to highjack what it means to be a man; but as a Christian, I believe it is my job as a parent to present God's concepts, values, and directives, whether they're currently popular or not.

Shielding *a* Boy's Heart

I was working with a recently divorced mother of three, whose youngest child is a boy. The state her life was in presented an emotional minefield that was treacherous and exhausting. Her relationship with her oldest daughter had turned rocky a few years earlier, in adolescence, and the divorce was placing a strain on their fragile interactions. Her middle daughter had recently taken to spending inordinate amounts of time in her room or on the phone. This mother seemed to take the withdrawal of her daughters a bit more in stride, assuming the divorce was going to be a rough transition for everyone, but the girls would eventually come around to her.

The bulk of her concern centered on her son, who was eight. According to her, they'd always been close, even closer than she was with the girls. She called him her "little man" and spoke affectionately about the bond between them. That bond, however, appeared to be changing. She was concerned he was "choosing sides" between her and her ex-husband. Tearful, she talked about what would happen if she "lost" him to his father.

As I probed for specifics of this "lost" behavior, she said he seemed more standoffish; he didn't want to snuggle as much anymore. She said he used to be so chatty about what he was doing and how he was feeling, but now he wasn't. She worried that he was still sharing with his father but not with her. He seemed to demand more privacy and became upset if she walked into his room too quickly, even after knocking. He never used to do that, she told me. What if, at some point, he decided he wanted to spend more time with his father and less with her?

■ ■ ■

In the midst of a season of profound change and loss, this mother was jumping to conclusions, leap-frogging to losing her son. The "evidence" she presented didn't indicate he was moving away from her as much as he was moving away from being a small child. An eight-year-old boy is not four or five. Those three or four years can make a big difference.

"Many mothers notice changes between five years old and ten years old in the way their sons process feelings and take care of their emotional needs."[19] These changes in emotional processing can be misinterpreted and taken personally, instead of viewed as the natural progression of maturing. As a small boy moves toward becoming an older boy, his body will change, and the way he deals with emotions will change. This change occurs even before he enters puberty. This eight-year-old, maturing boy was beginning to process his emotions differently, catching this distressed mom unaware.

Talk About It *or* Fix It?

Traditionally, it was believed that men and women dealt with emotions differently because that reflected the different ways we were raised. However, scientific research now indicates that there are two different emotional systems at work and that men rely on one, while women rely on the other.[20] To simplify, we'll call one the Talk-About-It mode and the other the Fix-It mode. Chances are, you already know which system women rely on and which system men prefer!

Let's break down the differences:

	TALK-ABOUT-IT MODE	FIX-IT MODE
CHARACTERIZATION	Emotional empathy	Cognitive empathy
DEFINITION	The capacity to enter into and feel another person's pain	The capacity to enter into analysis mode and develop a plan to fix the situation
GENDER (THAT RELIES MORE HEAVILY ON THIS MODE)	Female	Male

I've seen this difference played out in couples' counseling for years. A woman comes in, absolutely frustrated with her husband because she thinks he's uncaring. Why? As soon as she starts expressing her distress about a situation, he shuts her down by going into Fix-It mode. She'll be incensed that he thinks she's incapable of handling the situation on her own. She'll tell me, "I don't need him to fix it; I just need him to listen!"

What she fails to factor in, according to researchers, is that he does care. His initial response is emotional empathy. However, he doesn't stay there. Instead, he moves on to cognitive empathy, using a different brain system. Using emotional empathy, he is able to recognize and resonate with her pain. Once that reality is established, he moves on to utilizing his cognitive empathy, his Fix-It mode, in an attempt to find a solution to the problem. His response, though different, is not uncaring. Rather, he is attempting to analyze the situation, so he can find a way to fix it. To him, the way to alleviate the pain is to address it. To her, the way to alleviate the pain is to talk about it. Two very different approaches.

■ DON'T MISINTERPRET PROBLEM-SOLVING FOR LACK OF EMOTIONS.

A boy feels the same range of emotions that girls do; he may, however, simply move away from emotions in order to find a solution to what is causing the emotions. For example, a boy may be playing a game of basketball with friends and be teased because he missed every single shot. His answer may not be to run home and talk about the sting of humiliation. Instead, his answer may be to spend hours outside shooting the ball until he gets better.

■ ALLOW HIM TO DEFER TALKING.

There will come a time when he's ready to talk about strong and intense emotions he feels, but that time may be further out than you think. Allow him to choose when and where to talk. Demanding he open up may only provoke him to shut down.

■ TRY STARTING WITH THE SOLUTION AND NOT WITH THE PROBLEM.

In order for him to feel safe to talk, try tapping into his analyzing mode, focusing first on questions about what he needs to know to find his solution. Compliment him on his dedication to his basketball skills and mention how much better he's become. Then work into what caused the need to spend those hours at the hoop in the first place. End with other questions and actions he might take to solve the problem, bringing him back into Fix-It mode.

Take Action

Most men, in my experience, would rather have a root canal than go to a therapist. The thought of sitting for an hour in a chair talking about feelings is nightmarish.

In a strange way, sometimes I've found the only way to get a man I'm counseling to turn on his brain is to activate his body. Some of my best counseling sessions with men have taken place far from my office. I've counseled men while running in the neighborhood, hiking up a mountain, biking to the beach, walking to go get coffee.

SOMETIMES THE ONLY WAY TO GET A MAN TO TURN ON HIS BRAIN IS TO ACTIVATE HIS BODY.

Not only do these venues allow for the male brain to do what it appears to do well—connect perception to action—but it also provides the large space males may need to express themselves physically. A man who would stay emotionally closed sitting in an office chair may release his emotional energy through waving his arms or sprinting ahead. Intense emotional expression can be accompanied by intense physical expression. By moving into the great outdoors, space is provided for that synergistic expression (to say nothing of potentially saving my office décor).

■ GIVE HIM SPACE.

A boy is wired for action. In the midst of intense emotions, he may react physically. He may slam a door, wave his arms, or slap a table. As long as these expressions are not personally directed, allow him some space to physically react.

■ GIVE HIM TIME.

This concept bears repeating. When a boy is in the throes of a physical response to intense emotions, asking him to shut down that nuclear reactor so that he can sit still and talk is unrealistic. Depending upon his age (and the weather), get him outside. Play a game. Let him run the bases. Take the dog out for a walk. Go on an errand. Get him out and moving.

Recognize *the* Signs *of* Being Overwhelmed

I'll never forget a time one of my sons lost a football game. He was in middle school, and I was the resident taxi, driving back and forth to practices and games. Usually, these drive times were great bonding times for us, but after this particular loss, my son was completely shut down. Instead of giving him room, space, and time—all of the things I just said—I went right into therapist mode of asking Twenty Questions. Rather than opening up communication, I effectively shut it down. My thirteen-year-old was ill prepared to participate in a psychological breakdown of the emotional intensity of his loss. By barraging him with questions, I contributed to his sense of being overwhelmed.

I've heard something similar from men, especially when they feel pressured by the women in their lives to "open up." Women can intuitively feel that something is wrong and, quite naturally, seek to create the same situation that works so well with their female friends— get together and talk about it. This approach works well with women, who can be more verbally adept as well as being better wired to maintain a state of emotional empathy. This approach may not work as well with men who are so overwhelmed by what they're feeling, they can't begin to put a name to it, let alone spend an hour talking about it.

From what I've been able to read and observe over the course of my personal and professional life, a male can reach a point of bewilderment where emotions are concerned. Sometimes, he doesn't have the words he needs to explain or express what he's feeling. Sometimes, he's so used to suppressing intense emotions, he hasn't learned how to express them in safety.

When a male feels under siege by a demand to do the impossible—express or deal with what he cannot—the results aren't generally positive. He may become hostile, uncooperative, or defensive. None of these are helpful to having a discussion. When a man shuts down long enough, he can become estranged from his own emotions and find himself at even more of a loss to do what's being asked of him. When a boy is overwhelmed by an emotional response, you may need to strategize how to help him connect with and work through those feelings.

■ UNDERSTAND CAVE DWELLING.

I will be forever grateful to author John Gray for his book *Men Are from Mars, Women Are from Venus*.[21] It was Dr. Gray who, as far as I know, first coined the phrase "cave dwelling" for what boys and men do when they need to get away. Boys who hang out for hours in tree houses and rickety forts often are cave dwelling. Boys who practically live under the hood of old cars often are doing the same. A cave-dwelling boy can spend hours reading books in his room or playing video games. When a boy cave dwells, he's not hiding *from* his feelings, he's hiding *for* his feelings.

- ### GET OUT OF A ROUTINE BY ESTABLISHING ONE.

A boy who is overwhelmed emotionally can get into a rut of staying in his cave too long—out of avoidance, anger, or frustration. While you want to give him time to get a handle on his emotions, there comes a point when the boy may need help to come out. One man I knew would take his son out to fix something in the garage. They'd rearrange the tools on the shelves. They'd open up the hood of the car, tinker around, or change the oil or a filter. The point was to get his son out of the house, moving, and, hopefully, talking. At some point, his son caught on to the routine and made jokes about their "garage time."

■ ALLOW TEARS, BUT DON'T REQUIRE THEM.

One of the human reactions to being overwhelmed is to cry. Girls may tend to cry more easily, but boys can and do cry when they are overwhelmed. Just watch for the interviews at the end of the next big playoff game; you will see large, grown men shedding tears, whether they've won or lost.

● Both males and females cry, but their tears are different. "Women are biologically wired to shed tears more than men. Under a microscope, cells of female tear glands look different than men's. Also, the male tear duct is larger than the female's, so if a man and a woman both tear up, the woman's tears will spill onto her cheeks quicker."[22]

- As a therapist, I know that tears are natural and, sooner or later, they will come. Later is not always good, but later is usually better than never. Pent-up feelings of being overwhelmed by sadness, frustration, anger, or despair can lead to significant physical stress. In my business, the shedding of tears is often a healthy release and sign of a needed psychological breakthrough.

THE SHEDDING OF TEARS IS OFTEN A HEALTHY RELEASE AND SIGN OF A NEEDED PSYCHOLOGICAL BREAKTHROUGH.

- Tears as a natural reaction should be neither encouraged nor discouraged. Tears should be simply accepted when they happen.

- One of my favorite verses in Scripture is John 11:35, "Jesus wept." In this instance, Jesus is grieving the death of his friend Lazarus. I appreciate this verse, because it affirms tears as an appropriate male response to intense emotions.

■ READ A STORY.

A boy who is unable to figure out how he feels may be able to identify his feelings in someone else. The Bible is full of real-life stories with real-life emotions. If a boy is being picked on at school by a bully, read the story of Joseph and his brothers. If he's feeling unappreciated and misunderstood, read the story of Elijah. If he's facing a challenge too big for him, read the story of David and Goliath. A boy may not even realize he feels the same way until he puts himself in place of that character. The story acts as a bridge between the boy and his emotions.

Know *the* Seat *of* Emotions

The seat of emotions is not the heart; the seat of emotions is the brain. It seems logical to me that if male and female brains have differences, then male and female emotional responses will have differences. Over the years, I've been amused to see how often women believe their methods of processing emotions are superior to men and vice versa. I suppose we resonate with what we know. However, I've also known men who cried at the drop of a hat and women who fast-forwarded into Fix-It mode. I believe it's always important to remember these gender differences run across a spectrum.

The goal of understanding these differences isn't to judge one gender superior to the other but to increase awareness that differences exist. Because a boy may not react emotionally as a girl would doesn't mean there is something wrong with him. Because he may go into Fix-It mode or cave dwell, he is not emotionally stunted. Because he may express emotions physically does not mean he's destined to become abusive. As Christians, our job isn't to judge others; our job is to understand and, ultimately, to love one another, male and female, within the diversity created by God.

KEY #4:

Overseeing *a* Boy's Academics

Boys today are falling behind girls academically. This reversal of fortunes over the past fifty years is not confined to the United States. Prior to that, girls rarely went as far in school as boys, and boys were far more likely to graduate from college. But that's all changed. "In just a couple of generations, one gender gap has closed, only for another to open up."[23]

Here are some features of the new gender gap:

- In thirty-five developed countries, girls performed better on educational tests than boys did overall and particularly in reading and writing.[24]

- Educational policy has focused on encouraging females to achieve in the areas of math and science. However, the gender gaps in these areas are small, especially compared to the substantial gap for males in the areas of reading and writing.

■ The underachievement of boys in the areas of reading and writing can create a serious drawback for success in college as well as employment.[25]

■ Girls get higher grades than boys across all school subjects and enter college with high grade-point averages. Though boys typically receive higher test scores than girls in subjects such as math and science, girls still get better grades in school. (This difference may be due, at least in part, to the next point.)

- Girls are more likely to do homework, come to class prepared, participate in classroom activities, seek help, ask questions, and in other ways comply with classroom rules.

- Girls are more likely to go to college and graduate school, and those who do go are more likely to graduate. "In 2013, 25- to 34-year-old women were 21 percent more likely than men to be college graduates and 48 percent more likely to have completed graduate school."[26]

- Lack of success in school will continue to follow boys into manhood, affecting their ability to succeed at jobs and in other areas as well.[27]

The following comparisons between boys and girls are from Michael Gurian's book *The Minds of Boys*.[28]

ISSUE	BOYS	GIRLS
Receives the majority of Ds and Fs in school	✕	
Has the majority of discipline problems in school	✕	
Has the majority of children diagnosed with learning disabilities	✕	
Has the majority of children diagnosed with behavioral disorders	✕	
Has the majority of children on Ritalin or some similar drug	✕	
Is an average of one to one and a half years behind the other gender in reading and writing	✕	
Has the majority of high-school dropouts	✕	

Needless to say, this is not good news. Global evidence strongly indicates that the academic pendulum is swinging to the detriment of boys, with long-term negative consequences for higher education and employment. As society grapples with this concept of a boy crisis, individual boys and families struggle to find ways to succeed academically, my own family included.

The good news is there are steps adults can take to help navigate a boy's passage through academia. The following suggestions are those I've gleaned from my work, as well as from experiences my wife and I have gained by working with our sons. These suggestions are in no way meant as an exhaustive list but as a way for you to consider what you can do to help a boy succeed in school.

Do Your Part *at* School

■ ACTIVELY ENGAGE.

There might have been a day when all an adult had to do was drop a boy off at the school sidewalk in order to provide for his education. But not anymore. Those who are parenting boys should accept the responsibility to become active participants in their boys' educational experience.

- **Get to know his teachers.** This is much easier in grade school, because the number of teachers your child interacts with will be smaller, but don't let yourself off the hook in middle and high school. Remember, boys tend to disengage from education during middle school and drop out in high school, so you will need to remain vigilant from K-12. His teachers may be the first to recognize signs that he's struggling and can be valuable allies in the effort to re-engage him in school.

- **Attend curriculum nights, school activities, and parent-teacher conferences.** Believe me, I recognize these are more events to add to your already busy calendar, but each is important, because your attendance sends the message that you value education and are interested in his school and in his academic progress.

- **Whenever possible, volunteer at the school or in the classroom.** If you are at work during school hours, you can find ways to volunteer for after-school or weekend events. Volunteering also allows you to interact with other parents who can provide information about how the boys in their families are doing.

■ BE A POSITIVE PRESENCE.

The information presented here on boys might cause some adults to want to storm the gates, perceiving the neighborhood school as an academic battleground where males are concerned. I have felt that way myself a time or two over the years with my own sons. While I felt justified in my disappointment, anger, or frustration at how one of my sons was being treated or perceived, I couldn't let those feelings dictate my interactions with school staff. If you show up like a fire-breathing dragon every time you enter the building, school staff may run for cover, and your ability to address

> When the attitude of the adults take center stage, the problems of the boy may be upstaged.
>
> "IF IT IS POSSIBLE, AS FAR AS IT DEPENDS ON YOU, LIVE AT PEACE WITH EVERYONE."
> —ROMANS 12:18

your issues will be compromised. The staff you must work with at the school may react to you with irritation, frustration, or anger of their own.

■ COME WITH SOLUTIONS, NOT JUST PROBLEMS.

The ability to spot problems is much easier, I've found, than the ability to spot solutions. Yet when a boy has problems in school, the goal is to find workable, practical, and effective solutions. For example, the boy may not be reading up to grade level. The teacher has control over what happens perhaps twenty-five hours per week in that boy's life, but you may have at least as much, and probably more, time that you control. Suggest ways you can add to the classroom efforts to increase your boy's reading level and work with his teacher to coordinate your efforts.

■ EXCHANGE NOTES WITH OTHER PARENTS.

Boys may not always be forthcoming about problems with the atmosphere or environment of their classrooms. They may be struggling to adhere to classroom rules or with how the academic content is presented. If one boy in a classroom is having difficulty, it's possible that others are, as well. While you're helping out at the Harvest Carnival or standing on the sidelines during a game, engage other parents in conversation about the school in general, and, where applicable, about a specific classroom.

■ PROVIDE CONCRETE EXAMPLES.

If you do feel compelled to talk with a teacher or school administrator about the possibility of a classroom atmosphere that is mismatched for how boys learn, I highly suggest you bring in concrete examples from your experience and, whenever possible, the experience of other parents and boys. The natural tendency for people is to disregard what is considered criticism. In my experience, the more generalized and unsupported your observations, the less likely they are to be taken seriously. However, when you can provide specific incidents, patterns, behaviors, and consequences, you demonstrate you've done your homework and increase the likelihood you'll be heard.

■ PROVIDE INFORMATION.

When my book *Raising Boys by Design* was released, I made sure all of the staff at the Christian school where my sons attend received a complimentary copy. Likewise, this book and any of the works cited in the notes section at the end of this book are excellent materials that speak directly to teachers and instructional leaders. I earnestly believe the majority of teachers are well meaning and dedicated to their mission of education. Like all of us, they can struggle to keep up with the latest information and may not be aware of the ramifications of instructional practices on gender learning.

■ BE PERSISTENT BUT PLEASANT.

I would love it if every time I had a problem, I just needed to talk about it once to have it resolved. That so rarely happens. Don't expect any concerns you bring up at a single parent-teacher conference to solve the issue. Many school-related concerns will require monitoring and persistent engagement by you. You may need to circle back over weeks or months to create lasting change. In your persistency, remember to be pleasant and polite. These are people you need to work with and want in your corner where it comes to the boy in your life.

Do Your Part *at* Home

Boys can learn to succeed, even in difficult situations, when they have the support and understanding they need at home. Those of us parenting and mentoring boys should recognize the role we play in setting the stage academically by the family priorities and practices we establish at home.

BOYS CAN LEARN TO SUCCEED, EVEN IN DIFFICULT SITUATIONS.

- **ACCEPT RESPONSIBILITY TO BE HIS FIRST AND BEST TEACHER.**

  Those of us who parent boys need to understand that their education is not the sole responsibility of

any teacher or school. We should not abdicate our responsibility to be a boy's first and best teacher. What this means to me is that I continue to monitor what my sons are learning and how those lessons are being taught, and actively engage my sons in integrating family values and priorities into their educational content.

■ MAKE HOMEWORK A PRIORITY.

Boys may prefer to play video games over working on their spelling list. (I understand this temptation completely as I'd much rather sit and watch YouTube than go through my mail.) In our household, homework comes first. This rule supports the value my wife and I place in our sons' education. In my experience, homework left to the very end of the night does not produce my sons' best efforts. You may need to remove the gaming console, computer, or the power cords until homework is done.

■ LEAVE HIM SOME BREATHING ROOM.

While I don't think it's a good idea to hold homework until the very end of the evening, I also don't think it works well to chain him to his desk right after school. My thought is you should use the Goldilocks Rule for homework: not too early and not too late. After sitting for hours at school, a boy may need time to be outside, to run around and play, to get all his energy and wiggles out, before he's ready to sit back down and concentrate on his homework.

■ MAKE ROOM FOR MOVEMENT.

If sitting in a classroom doesn't work well for a boy, sitting at a kitchen table probably won't either. A boy may need to move around while doing his homework or in order to avoid zoning out. One suggestion is to use a stress ball or other object that can be squeezed or tossed as a way to integrate movement into sitting time. For example, if a boy is learning his multiplication tables or state capitals, you might throw a Nerf ball back and forth to him, requiring him to provide a correct answer every time he catches the

ball. This game introduces competition into his learning and can help motivate him to accomplish what he might otherwise find tedious or boring.

■ ORGANIZE HIS EFFORTS.

Schoolwork can be presented as a series of tasks that must be systematically addressed and conquered. Especially when a boy gets into middle school and begins to have multiple classes and multiple teachers, helping him find a way to organize his work can be worthwhile. This could be a paper-and-pencil planner or an application where he (and you) can track what he has to do and when it is due. Initially, you'll probably need to keep tight tabs on how this is going, but as he proves successful and trustworthy, you should be able to stand down from being the Planner Police.

■ BUT DON'T DO IT FOR HIM.

Struggling with homework is not necessarily a bad thing. Boys need to be challenged and tested. Watch to make sure he is making progress, even if he exhibits frustration or complains. Your role should be to support him, not supplant him, where homework is concerned.

■ MONITOR THE DISTRACTIONS.

If it were up to many boys, they would be on their phones, listening to music at ear-splitting decibels, and intermittently playing a video game while doing homework. I remember vividly trying to convince my parents that, really, doing three things at once while I was doing my homework resulted in amazing productivity. They didn't buy it and neither should you.

BOYS NEED TO BE CHALLENGED AND TESTED.

■ BRING IN REINFORCEMENTS.

At some point, even the most amenable boy may become tired of the same person insisting on the same rules, doing things the same way. If you're able, change up the adults working with the boy. If Dad's been taking the bulk of the duty, bring in Mom. If Mom's been on-task for a while, see if an older brother or sister could help. What about a nearby relative, like an aunt, uncle, or grandparent? The more adults (or older teenagers) that commit to supporting a boy's education, the more invested he may become himself, as he seeks to please those he loves and respects. If he persists in significant learning difficulties, consider having him meet with a professional tutor. Use a sports analogy and call that person a coach instead of a tutor.

■ FUEL HIM UP.

A boy learns best when he's well nourished. I know this sounds simplistic, but as a parent, I understand how hard it is to accomplish. My sons can be like mini-tornadoes going through my kitchen cupboards, consuming everything in sight. They are often not concerned with nutritional content, just filling up the empty pit inside. As much as you are able, I encourage you to have healthy snacks and food for him to eat. The better the fuel, the better the performance. Send him off to school nutritionally well prepared by providing both the time for and the components of a good breakfast.

■ HELP HIM REST.

Boys are active, and active bodies that need downtime. For this reason, at the Jantz household, we do not allow televisions in bedrooms. Our electronics are stored in a common area, recharging at night when we are. Children, including teenagers, need their sleep to perform well. A tired boy cannot do his best.

Be *His* Academic Quarterback

You may not be providing the bulk of a boy's academic content, but you can certainly still oversee his education. He may have outside teachers, paraeducators, or coaches working with him, but you remain his academic quarterback. He will need your guidance, oversight, and assistance all the way through his graduation from high school and onto whatever world he enters next, be it vocational, military, technical, or academic.

Each boy needs someone on the sidelines cheering him on, who isn't timid about stepping onto the field, when necessary, to have his back. He needs to understand the importance and the mission of education and its value to his life in the moment and in the future. The disturbing statistics about the current state of boys, in school and in life, will only be turned around and improved one boy at a time.

KEY #5:

Educating *a* Boy About Sex

Do you remember your mom or dad giving you "the talk" back when you were a kid? Mine took place right before we moved from Kansas to Idaho, when I was in the sixth grade. My mom said she wanted to talk to me and we ended up seated at the kitchen table. I knew something was up. Armed with a book she'd gotten at a Christian bookstore, she proceeded to explain how sex worked, in an embarrassing version of "label the body parts." In a state of semi-shock at hearing about this from my mother, I asked no questions and got up from the table as soon as possible.

After we moved that year to Idaho, I fell in at school with a rough crowd who seemed to talk of little else but girls and sex. There was one boy, at the end of my block, who helpfully provided a different sort of graphic presentation of "the talk," this one via glossy, centerfold magazines. Not at all the sort of education my mother had in mind.

■ ■ ■

Ask a group of adult friends about where they learned about sex, and you're sure to get a variety of grimaces and responses. Some might say their parents never did clue them in. Instead, their wealth of knowledge came from sources like mine: clandestine schoolyard conversations and stolen issues of male magazines. Some may have survived a health class in school—if one was offered— and gotten some level of factual information. A few may admit to frank and open discussion with parents that took place over a series of years, but I've found those to be few and far between. Why is that? Why are we so fearful to explain one of God's amazing gifts?

> Why are we so fearful to explain one of God's amazing gifts?
>
> "GOD CREATED MANKIND IN HIS OWN IMAGE, IN THE IMAGE OF GOD HE CREATED THEM; MALE AND FEMALE HE CREATED THEM."
> —GENESIS 1:27

I've been saddened by the number of Christians I've spoken with who have related feelings of mortification and shame around learning of their God-designed anatomies. Instead of understanding their bodies and sexual expression as a divinely positive gift, they have been presented with a negative view fraught with danger and shame. The message they've received is similar to the unfortunate one I got at my kitchen table: Sex is a gift from God, but sex is dangerous. If you use it wrong, you're going to hell.

Here are some statistics from a recent study done with U.S. high-school students by the Centers for Disease Control and Prevention. By age nineteen:

- 53 percent have had sexual intercourse.

- 34 percent were sexually active during the previous three months and of those, four in ten did not use a condom during their last sexual encounter.

- 15 percent have had sex with four or more people.

- Less than a fourth of the sexually experienced had been tested for HIV, even though almost ten thousand young people (ages eleven to twenty-four) were diagnosed with HIV in the U.S. in 2013.

- Almost half of the twenty million new cases of sexually transmitted diseases (STDs) diagnosed each year were in those aged fifteen to twenty-four.

- In 2013, about 273,000 babies were born to teenage girls aged fifteen to nineteen.[29]

To an emerging adolescent, either male or female, sex doesn't necessarily seem dangerous—weird, perhaps, but not dangerous. Instead, sex can seem exciting, pleasurable, and grown-up. In short, a negative message can appear to be out of sync with the positive realities a boy may experience. In the face of this contradiction, he may decide to pay more attention to the positives he feels than to the negatives he's told.

Help *Him* Navigate *His* Sexuality

Within this labyrinth of positives and negatives, how is a boy—and the adults in his life—to navigate an explanation about God's gift of and design for sex? The following are some suggestions I've gleaned from my own life experiences, my being the parent of boys, and my years of talking with men and women.

■ BE PREPARED FOR HIS SEXUALITY.

Prepuberty begins at around nine years of age. From that point on, your son is dealing with five to seven testosterone spikes per day. This means his body and brain are dealing with these chemicals; and the results can be moodiness, pimples, aggression, gangliness, impulsivity, new body and facial hair, a squeaky voice, innovation, creativity, intensity, and even brilliance.[30]

If you are an adult raising maturing boys, I encourage you not to try to avoid the inevitable but to be prepared to deal with sexuality head-on. Instead of considering his coming-of-age sexually as something to dread, be ready to embrace this stage of his life—of your life together—in a positive, encouraging, and spiritually based way. His sexuality—and how he navigates it with your help—will set the

> How he navigates his sexuality with your help will set the direction for his path to adulthood.
>
> "START CHILDREN OFF ON THE WAY THEY SHOULD GO, AND EVEN WHEN THEY ARE OLD THEY WILL NOT TURN FROM IT."
> —PROVERBS 22:6

direction for his path to adulthood and manhood going forward. "Start children off on the way they should go, and even when they are old they will not turn from it" (Proverbs 22:6).

■ PRESENT THE BODY AND SEXUALITY AS A DIVINE GIFT OF GOD.

Culture warps sexuality, perverting God's plan for the body. In the process of rejecting the sexuality encouraged by our culture, Christians often come across as rejecting sex itself and the sexual design of the bodies God made. This negative view of sex doesn't line up with reality. A boy is designed to experience pleasure from sexual expression. He is designed to react pleasurably to sexual stimuli. Adults should be truthful with boys about this reality and use it to explain sex as the wondrous gift from God that it is.

■ PRESENT THE CHALLENGE OF RESPONSIBILITY.

Boys love a good challenge. And sexual purity is a good challenge. I believe a boy needs to know that his sexuality is a precious gift from God. And, as with many precious gifts, there is a responsibility to use the gift wisely. To borrow a superhero metaphor, Superman and Spiderman are given gifts of immense power. Each of these superheroes has plot lines where he is tempted to use his gifts selfishly but must overcome that temptation in order to use the gift not for harm but for good. The potency of sex is like having a superpower, and boys can be challenged to respond heroically by learning to control this power for good.

BOYS LOVE A GOOD CHALLENGE. AND SEXUAL PURITY IS A GOOD CHALLENGE.

■ **START EARLY.**

In *The Wonder of Boys,* the author relates a story about "the talk" he had with his father. Basically, this three-sentence conversation consisted of two questions and a comment:

"You know about sex, right?"

"And you know if you have questions you can come to me, right?"

"Okay, then. Just be careful. Sex isn't something to mess with."[31]

Did you notice the assumption in the first question? I wonder how many other adults have waited to have "the talk" until after they were sure someone else had beat them to it. Believe me, a boy will hear sexual information from many sources, especially now with so many options available through technology. If you want to have influence, you may need to jump that line to be first. Start discussing sexuality and genitalia early, in age-appropriate ways. If you're unclear what is considered age-appropriate, do what my mom did and get a trusted book (just don't bring it to the kitchen table).

■ HAVE TALKS—NOT JUST ONE TALK.

Teaching about sexuality should be like teaching anything else related to God. The Bible says spiritual concepts need to be always front and center: "Teach them to your children, talking about them when you sit at home and when you walk along the road, when you lie down and when you get up" (Deuteronomy 11:19). I encourage you to find times and places when you can naturally engage in sexual teaching with the boy in your life, not just a one-time kitchen-table talk.

Talk About Sex *in an* Age-Appropriate Manner[32]

AGE	POINTS TO DISCUSS
2	It's best to avoid cutesy names for genitalia. It is better to call a penis a penis, the way you call a nose a nose. Some people prefer terms such as "private parts" or, more generically, "crotch."
3 TO 5	■ Continue correctly labeling body parts and begin discussing good touching versus bad touching. Let your son know that certain body parts are only for touching by themselves, by mom and dad, and by the doctor for reasons of health and cleanliness. ■ If your child asks where babies come from, it's best to answer truthfully, but avoid a full-on obstetrics lecture. Give as much truthful information as possible to answer the question. "A mommy has an egg and the daddy has a seed. The egg and seed come together in a place called the mommy's 'womb,' and a baby grows there." Supply similar answers to any follow-up questions your child may have.

6 TO 8	Inform your son about the changes that will be happening to his body. If you wait for your son to come to you with questions, you may wait forever. Your silence on the matter may communicate to him that sex is a forbidden topic.
9 TO 12	■ Reassure your son that all the strange things happening to his body (acne, wet dreams, masturbation, cracking voice, body and facial hair) are perfectly normal and something every man experiences.
	■ This is the age that kids find porn on the Internet or are offered access to porn at the homes of their friends. Make sure they understand what you want them to do when these situations arise. Make sure they understand your reasons and the risks that accompany the use of pornography.
	■ Talk about the physical and emotional risks of becoming sexually active at a young age.

13 TO 18	■ Make sure your child knows that even though our culture makes it look like everyone is having sex, not all young people are sexually active. It's okay to be celibate.
	■ Continue your discussions regarding masturbation, pornography, birth control, and any other topic that presents itself. Not all talks have to be long discussions. Some can be a quick reply in response to something in a discussion, television show, song, etc.
19 AND OLDER	Continue to discuss healthy sexual relations with your son as he continues to grow and enter new phases of life: going off to college, moving to a new city, getting married, and even when he's old enough to begin having conversations with his own children.

■ EXPECT EXPERIMENTATION.

Most boys, as they approach puberty, will masturbate. One study I saw reported almost 63 percent of fourteen-year-old males had masturbated at least once; and by the age of seventeen, 80 percent had. The frequency also rose with age, with around 43 percent of fourteen-year-old males reporting masturbating within the previous month, while almost 68 percent of seventeen-year-olds had. [33]

Before people began to do actual studies, the old adage I remember hearing was 98 percent of people masturbate and the other 2 percent are lying. Expect experimentation, and determine ahead of time how you want to broach this subject. I found the following advice to parents from the Focus on the Family website to be helpful:

> "We believe it's vital to resist the temptation to overreact to this situation, and we would strongly urge you to avoid heaping guilt on your teenager over this issue. Adolescents are in the process of discovering their own sexuality, and many of them find the urge to masturbate almost uncontrollable. They may be driven to despair over this issue if parents

convey an overly harsh or critical perspective. Instead of worrying and becoming upset, then, we'd advise you to turn this situation into an opportunity to explore the Biblical view of sex with your child—tactfully and sensitively, of course."[34]

If you haven't already worked through how you feel about masturbation—as it relates to you, as you understand it in the context of sexuality and Scripture, as it relates to others—I encourage you to do so. In order to be prepared to mentor a boy on this important subject, you first need to know and be able to explain what you believe and why.

■ PROVIDE MALE MENTORING.

I'm not sure if I wished my dad had given me "the talk" instead of my mom or if I'd rather neither of them had given it. But that's just me. I know there are many mothers who handle the sex talk with their sons better than the fathers could have. And there are many single moms who don't have the option to have dad step in. However, I suspect most boys, if given a choice, would prefer to talk to a guy about guy stuff. I don't mean this to disregard women; but, as a man raising sons, I have experienced and seen that "there are times when a boy needs another man to teach him how to be a good man."[35]

This is especially true for boys being raised by single mothers, particularly divorced mothers. Too often, anger at the former spouse can turn into anger at all men—for the mother, the son, or both! If you are a divorced mom, please don't let any unresolved issues with your ex-husband cause you to say bad things about him to your son. And especially don't make statements about all men being bad. Remember, your son is growing into a man. If your son can find a mentor to take an interest in him, do everything in your power to encourage the relationship.

As a father, I want to be that male mentor for my sons, but I recognize that they can learn from other trusted men, as well. Boys can be mentored by fathers, by older brothers, uncles, grandfathers, fathers of friends, male youth pastors, men from a faith community. For those boys being predominantly raised by females, I believe that at least one male mentor—one who has been prescreened and with whom some preplanning has been done—should be provided.

Ideally, this male mentor can instruct a boy on a variety of male issues—how to operate in male culture, what a good man looks and acts like, how to be on the watch for and avoid male temptations, how and why to treat females with respect—not just sexuality. Again, a good male mentor can tailor these lessons to be age-appropriate and to take place naturally over the course of months, if not years.

Emphasize God's View *of* Sex

Educating a boy about sex is really about educating a boy about life. He was designed by God as a sexual being, and that sexuality is not something negative or dangerous, only to be delved into cautiously with suspicion and shame as an adult. I want boys to understand that sexuality is a reality of God's design for them that is right and good. I want boys to recognize that the physical pleasures and reactions are normal and part of their natural, biological design.

Further, I want boys to be taught that their sexuality should be appreciated, understood, and woven into the Creator's intention for sex and marriage. God has chosen marriage—and the sexual union marriage entails—as the earthly representation of God's relationship with us, his people (Isaiah 54:5). The church, after all, is the bride of Christ (Revelation 21:2). More than anything, I want sexuality wrestled out of the hands of culture and placed back in the hands of God, where it so rightly belongs.

SEXUALITY IS A REALITY OF GOD'S DESIGN THAT IS RIGHT AND GOOD.

Word *of* Encouragement

I could not end without a note of thanks to and a word of encouragement for those of you engaged in the exhilarating, frustrating, and sometimes controversial occupation of bringing up boys.

- First, thank you for wading into these issues with a willingness to learn, to grow, and, perhaps, to change an opinion or attitude.

- Thank you for being watchful of the condition of boys currently with an eye out to the horizon of manhood ahead.

- Thank you for loving the boys in your life enough to spend time with them, get to know them, and appreciate them for who they are and how they were created to be.

- Thank you for not shying away from, but celebrating, their differences. Boys need advocates that appreciate who they are.

By way of encouragement, I'd like you to consider learning more. Naturally, I recommend the books mentioned in this text already and those listed in the notes section at the end of this book. My hope is, as you've read over this material, you've underlined, scribbled in the margins, placed stars, and highlighted sections with specific insights you've gained and actions you can take to better the condition of the boys you know and love. I would love for that engagement in the development of boys to continue.

That Pesky Pendulum

Pendulums are interesting objects. "In a vacuum, once a pendulum is set in motion, it will continue swinging up to the same height from which it was released for an infinite amount of time. It will only change its course if some outside force acts on it."[36] I believe the current course of the pendulum for boys needs to change. I believe the outside force needed to create that change comes from each of us. Individually and collectively, relying on strength and wisdom from God, we can make individual decisions and take individual actions toward a better understanding of and appreciation for boys—their natures and their needs.

Notes

1. Gregory L. Jantz and Michael Gurian, *Raising Boys by Design: What the Bible and Brain Science Reveal About What Your Son Needs to Thrive* (Colorado Springs, CO: Waterbrook Press, 2013).

2. Michael Gurian, *Helping Boys Thrive* (October 2015), http://helpingboysthrive.org.

3. Anita Sethi, "The Real Difference Between Boys and Girls," *Parenting*, http://www.parenting.com/article/real-difference-between-boys-and-girls.

4. Renee Bacher, "Who's Easier: Boys or Girls?" *American Baby* (May 2004), http://www.parents.com/kids/development/social/boys-or-girls.

5. Holly Pevzner, "Ten Things I Wish I'd Known About Raising a Boy," *Today* (July 29, 2015), http://www.today.com/parents/10-things-i-wish-id-known-about-raising-boy-1D79911267.

6. Aline Weiller, "Got boys? What It's Like to Only Have Sons," *Brain Child* (April 18, 2013), http://www.brainchildmag.com/2013/04/got-boys-what-its-like-to-only-have-sons.

7. University of California, Irvine, "Intelligence in Men and Women Is a Gray and White Matter," *ScienceDaily* (January 22, 2005), www.sciencedaily.com/releases/2005/01/050121100142.htm.

8. Bill Farrel and Pam Farrel, *Men Are Like Waffles—Women Are Like Spaghetti* (Eugene, OR: Harvest House Publishers, 2001).

9. Kevin Schut, "Can God Fit in This Machine? Video Games and Christians," *Christian Research Institute*, https://www.equip.org/article/can-god-fit-in-this-machine-video-games-and-christians.

10. Madhura Ingalhalikar et al., "Sex Differences in the Structural Connectome of the Human Brain," *PNAS* (December 2, 2013): 823–828, doi: 10.1073/pnas.1316909110.

11. Joan Littlefield Cook and Greg Cook, "Similarities and Differences Between Boys and Girls." *Child Development Principles and Perspectives (Boston: Pearson, 2009).*

12. Simon Baron-Cohen, Rebecca C. Knickermeyer, and Matthew K. Belmonte, "Sex Differences in the Brain: Implications for Explaining Autism," *Science (November 4, 2005): 819–823, doi: 10.1126/science.1115455.*

13. Cook and Cook, "Similarities and Differences Between Boys and Girls."

14. "How Male and Female Brains Differ," *WebMD*, http://www.webmd.com/balance/features/how-male-female-brains-differ.

15. Cook and Cook, "Similarities and Differences Between Boys and Girls."

16. "How Male and Female Brains Differ," *WebMD*.

17. Thomas G. Mortenson, "The State of American Manhood," *Postsecondary Education Opportunity* (September 2006).

18. Jantz and Gurian, *Raising Boys by Design*, 86–87.

19. Michael Gurian, *The Wonder of Boys* (New York: Penguin Putnam, 1997): 20.

20. Louann Brizendine, *The Male Brain*, (New York: Three Rivers Press, 2010): 96–97.

21. John Gray, *Men Are from Mars, Women Are from Venus* (New York: HarperCollins Publishing, 1992).

22. Katherine Rosman, "Read It and Weep, Crybabies," *The Wall Street Journal* (May 4, 2011), http://www.wsj.com/articles/SB100014240527487039228045763009031835 12350.

23. "The Weaker Sex," *The Economist* (March 7, 2015), http://www.economist.com/news/international/21645759-boys-are-being-outclassed-girls-both-school-and-university-and-gap.

24. Michael Gurian, *The Minds of Boys* (San Francisco, CA: Jossey-Bass, 2005): 22–23.

25. Judith Kleinfeld, "The State of American Boyhood," *Gender Issues* (2009): 119, doi: 10.1007/s12147-009-9074-z.

26. Allie Bidwell, "Women More Likely to Graduate College, but Still Earn Less Than Men," *U.S. News and World Report* (October 31, 2014), http://www.usnews.com/news/blogs/

data-mine/2014/10/31/women-more-likely-to-graduate-college-but-still-earn-less-than-men.

27. Mortenson, "The State of American Manhood."

28. Michael Gurian, *The Wonder of Boys*, 22

29. "Sexual Risk Behaviors: HIV, STD, and Teen Pregnancy Prevention," *Centers for Disease Control and Prevention*, http://www.cdc.gov/healthyyouth/sexualbehaviors/index.htm.

30. Jantz and Gurian, *Raising Boys by Design*, 128.

31. Michael Gurian, *The Wonder of Boys*, 221.

32. Cheryl Embrett, "Age-by-Age Guide to Talking to Kids About Sex," *Today's Parent* (June 9, 2014), http://www.todaysparent.com/family/parenting/age-by-age-guide-to-talking-to-kids-about-sex.

33. Cynthia L. Robbins, et al., "Prevalence, Frequency, and Associations of Masturbation with Partnered Sexual Behaviors Among US Adolescents," *Archives of Pediatrics and Adolescent Medicine* (December 2011), doi: 10.1001/archpediatrics.2011.142.

34. "Talking to Your Teen About Masturbation," *Focus on the Family Canada* (2010), http://www.focusonthefamily.ca/parenting/teens/talking-to-your-teen-about-masturbation.

35. Jantz and Gurian, *Raising Boys by Design*, 128.

36. Grant D. McKenzie, "How Does a Pendulum Work?" *eHow*, http://www.ehow.com/how-does_4913131_a-pendulum-work.html.